AN INTERACTIVE WORKBOOK
FOR INDIVIDUAL OR SMALL-GROUP STUDY

you and me FOREVER
study guide

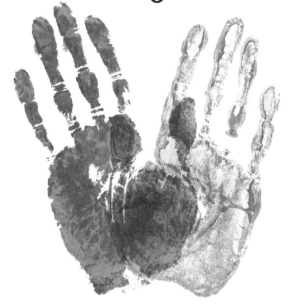

marriage in light of eternity

FRANCIS CHAN & LISA CHAN

WITH **MARK BEUVING**

you and me FOREVER study guide

Published by Claire Love Publishing
4100 3rd Street / San Francisco, CA 94124

ISBN: 978-0-9903514-3-6

Cover Design: Dann Petty
Hand Lettering: Jim Elliston
Typeset: Peter Gloege
Author Photo: Tamiz Photography

Printed in the United States of America
21 20 19 18 17 16 15 (DP) 10 9 8 7 6 5 4 3 2 1

CONTENTS

GETTING STARTED

I suspect that many people will be reading this for many different reasons. Some are experiencing difficulty in their marriage, and they're looking for a resource to help get their marriage back on track. Others are enjoying their marriages—things are going pretty smoothly—but they know there is more to marriage and want to dig deeper. Then there will be engaged or dating couples looking to plan ahead for their marriages, as well as single people who would someday like to be married.

I can picture a host of situations that would lead someone to study marriage in greater depth. But regardless of where you're coming from, your study of marriage should lead you to the same place. Namely, studying marriage should lead us to worship the God who created marriage.

Too often, Christians get so caught up in the concept of marriage, or in their specific marriages, that God fades to the background. Something that God created to bring glory to Himself becomes an obsession, a replacement for God, an idol. Lisa and I have seen many books and studies on marriage that focus so heavily on making marriages "work" better that they end up feeding into this idolatrous approach to marriage.

We're not claiming that this study on marriage will be perfect, but we want to challenge you to see marriage in light of the God who created it. We want you to see your marriage as a means of glorifying God, as an important part of the mission

He has given you on earth, as a way to love God more fully, and as a way of enjoying Him in this life.

The truth is, marriage is absolutely brilliant. Who could come up with such an incredible plan other than God? Our marriage is not perfect, but we love being married to each other, we love enjoying God's design for marriage, and we are absolutely committed to seeing our marriage be everything God wants it to be. Our goal with this study is to help you evaluate your own marriage (present or future) in light of eternity.

The most important thing you can do as you begin this study is pray. Commit to doing this study prayerfully. Don't try to strategize about your marriage, don't look for ways to manipulate your spouse, don't develop a wish list for what your current or future spouse should look like. Instead, do this study in the presence of God. Lay your plans and dreams for marriage at His feet. Don't look for your spouse to be changed; ask God to change you.

God designed you in a specific way for a specific purpose. If you are (or will be) married, that's because God's plan for you includes your marriage to that one specific person. God has a mission for His church, and that mission involves every single one of us. And if you're married, His mission involves your marriage. Whatever you do, don't waste your marriage on your own happiness. Don't sidetrack God's mission with your own dreams for marriage. God's mission is too important; your marriage is too significant.

So we invite you now, before you even begin this study, to let go. Let go of your plans for marriage. Let go of the changes you've been wanting to see in your marriage. Let go of your plans for your spouse, the hurt you've been harboring, the dream you've been pursuing. Let go of all of it and ask God to simply do what He wants done. Offer yourself to Him as a servant. Ask Him to change you and use you however He wants.

If you view your marriage as the most important thing in your life, you'll have a hard time letting go. But if you view marriage in light of eternity, as we will be challenging you to do, then letting go only makes sense. Your marriage isn't yours. Your life isn't your own. It's all about God. It's all about eternity. It's all about the mission He lovingly calls you into. Let's lay it all down for the sake of Jesus.

How To Get The Most Out Of This Workbook

There are a few ways to use this workbook. You can work through the study as an individual, as a couple, as a part of a small group, or even during a weekend retreat. You can use it before you're married as a form of premarital counseling, in the midst of a healthy marriage as a solid reminder and challenge, or in the midst of a troubled marriage that desperately needs to be reshaped according to Scripture. We have made some suggestions for using the workbook in each of these settings below.

This workbook is designed to work hand in hand with the book, *You & Me Forever*, and the videos that accompany each chapter. The book itself, along with all of the corresponding videos are available for free at youandmeforever.org. Ideally, you will read the relevant chapter from *You & Me Forever,* watch the appropriate video, then go through the corresponding session in this workbook.

Using the Workbook on Your Own

The most effective way to use this workbook is to go through it on your own, even if you're also going to discuss it as a couple, as a group, or on a retreat. In other words, make sure you apply the concepts directly to yourself. Many of the questions are personal, and taking the time to read through the sessions and think through how each question should affect your life will give the study depth and immediate personal application.

We suggest reading the corresponding chapter in *You & Me Forever* before starting each session of the workbook (if you don't have the book, it's available for free at youandmeforever.org). We also recommend watching the corresponding video for each chapter before you go through each session in this workbook. These videos will give you further challenges and provide some practical insight into each topic. The videos are free, and can be found online at youandmeforever.org.

Using the Workbook in Premarital Counseling

Many couples will want to use this study as a part of their premarital counseling. If that's you, we highly recommend that you use this study in conjunction with meeting with a pastor or leader in your church. Having a real relationship with a wise Christian in your church is invaluable, and he or she should be able to dive into your life in a way that no book ever could. If you're not part of a church, this is a great reason to join a healthy church in your area. If you're part of a church but don't know anyone that might discuss these concepts with you, try reaching out to a leader or administrator. Your church exists to help you grow; find out if they have any programs that might help you or leaders who could meet with you.

For premarital counseling, we recommend that you each work through one session at a time on your own (see the instructions for studying as an individual above), then meet together to discuss the content and your answers to the questions. Pay special attention to the areas where your answers differ. Communicating openly about these things will prepare you for marriage, and "arguing" well is great practice for working through the problems that will inevitably arise in your marriage.

If you are a pastor or leader in a church and want to use this material in premarital counseling for other couples, we recommend that you read each chapter in *You & Me Forever*, watch the corresponding video, and work through the material in this workbook. If this prompts any advice you'd like to give the couple or questions you'd like to ask them, great. You can also go through each question in the workbook and ask them both to respond and guide them in thinking through their answers. You can also ask them which questions they found most interesting or difficult, or which questions they disagreed on.

There is nothing entirely unique or magical in these pages or in the questions; the important thing is that you help each couple think deeply about marriage, its purpose, and the role that God calls each of them to play. You'll also want to use the wisdom God has given you to alert them to potential difficulties. However you decide to do that with each couple, be sure that you are actively depending on God for wisdom and actively praying for the couple through the process.

Using the Workbook in a Small Group

If you're working through the material as a part of a small group, the best way to begin is by working through each chapter on your own before the group discussion (see the section for individuals above). Reading and thinking through each session on your own before your group meets will better prepare you for the discussion. We recommend writing in your answers and any notes or questions you may have before you meet with your group, and then adding to your notes based on the discussion.

When you meet with your group, we recommend establishing a discussion leader. (If you've been chosen for this task, see the "Notes for Discussion Leaders" at the end of this workbook.) This person doesn't need to have all the answers. The discussion leader will simply guide the conversation and decide when to move on to the next question. Feel free to rotate the role of discussion leader week to week if this works better.

For each session, discuss the numbered questions as a group. We suggest jumping from one question to the next, but feel free to read a section out loud if the questions are unclear. Some of the questions can be answered quickly, but we encourage you to take your time, giving multiple group members a chance to share. This will enrich the discussion, and different perspectives will often give you more ideas for practical application.

We recommend that each group member read the appropriate chapter in *You & Me Forever* before your group discussion. That will give everyone more insight for the discussion. You will have to decide how your group will interact with the corresponding videos (available at youandmeforever.org). You may want to have each member watch the video before the meeting. This will enrich their preparation for the discussion. Or you may choose to watch the videos together as part of your group meeting. This will ensure that everyone sees the videos and that they're fresh on everyone's minds. If you choose to show the videos in your group time, we recommend watching the videos at the beginning to jumpstart your discussion. Whichever approach you choose, the videos will add a level of depth to your discussion, and since these videos have a practical emphasis, they should add to your application of the material. After watching the videos, you may simply start by asking, "What stood out to you from the video?" That may generate healthy discussion before you even approach the discussion questions.

Most importantly, we encourage you to be honest with the members of your group. If your desire is to grow and change, you will need the other group members to pray for you, support you, and at times challenge your thinking. By opening up to one another, your whole group will become more open to the Spirit's leading. And you will likely be surprised by the extent to which other group members share your struggles.

Using the Workbook for a Weekend Retreat

Some churches will want to use this workbook as a part of a weekend retreat. If that's the case, the retreat leaders have some decisions to make: Do you want to use the videos for all or part of the main sessions? Maybe you'll want to plan out messages around the material covered in each session (if that's the case, we highly recommend reading *You & Me Forever* first). You may just want to plan eight meeting times during the course of the weekend, play the videos for the whole group, and then have everyone break off into smaller groups to discuss the material.

However you choose to do it, we recommend dividing the large group into smaller groups and setting aside eight different small-group meeting times. Small groups of four to eight people give everyone a chance to talk. People who are shy about talking in large groups are often more comfortable talking in small ones. And people who tend to dominate discussions in large groups are more easily balanced out by others in small circles.

You'll probably want to address the entire group at least a few times during the weekend to give them some thoughts, but giving them time to meet in smaller groups will be important. Group members will want to read the section for small groups above, and discussion leaders will want to read the "Notes for Discussion Leaders" section at the end of this workbook.

Discussion leaders don't need to be experts either in the content or in leading groups, because they will fairly quickly learn how to guide a conversation with only four to eight other people. Ideally, you will choose discussion leaders ahead of time, but if you can't, it's surprising how often these groups can choose the most natural leader among them after getting to know each other for only a brief time. You can read aloud the job description of a discussion leader (see the end of this workbook) and pray for the Holy Spirit to guide the groups in choosing discussion leaders. Groups will often unanimously choose someone among them to do the job once they know what it involves.

It's a good idea for people to stick with the same group for the whole series, so that they get to know each other.

All of the videos are available at youandmeforever.org.

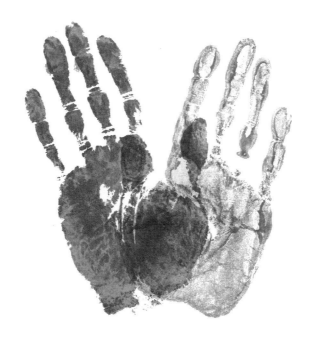

SESSION ONE

Marriage Isn't that Great

For more information on the material in this session,
read the Introduction and Chapter 1 of the book
You & Me Forever and take a few minutes to watch the
relevant video(s) at youandmeforever.org.

Everyone is familiar with marriage. Whether it's your own marriage, your parents', your friends', a pop-culture representation, or an idea of what your marriage will look like in the future, we all have deep-seated ideas about what marriage is and should be. You are probably far more opinionated about marriage than you think you are.

So before we look at what the Bible says about marriage, we have to evaluate our own assumptions about marriage. I'm not trying to tell you that everything you've ever thought about marriage is wrong. Nor am I suggesting that you probably have a horrible marriage. I simply want you to assess the way you think about marriage.

What makes for a good marriage? What is the purpose of marriage? What types of marriage have you seen? By honestly taking stock of our thoughts and feelings regarding marriage we can expose our assumptions and prepare ourselves to hear from God on the matter. Start by answering and discussing the questions below.

1. *Explain your experience with marriage up to this point. If you're married, briefly describe what marriage has been like. If you're engaged, describe what your relationship is like and how you expect your relationship to look once you're married. If you're not yet married, what expectations do you have about what marriage will be like (identify where these expectations come from—parents, friends, pastors, etc.)?*

2. *Answer one or both of the following questions: (1) What is the healthiest marriage you've seen? Why do you say that? (2) What is the unhealthiest marriage you've seen? (You don't have to use real names.) Why do you say that?*

Now that you've laid out some of your experiences with marriage—whether it's personal experience or what you've observed—it's time to put your view of marriage in biblical perspective.

As with any issue, many of our assumptions about marriage need to change. Marriage was God's idea. It functions according to His design. It doesn't matter what your parents' marriage is like. It doesn't matter how your culture portrays marriage. It doesn't matter how your marriage has functioned to this point or how you dream your marriage could look. Ultimately, all that matters is what God says about marriage.

Before we dive into the biblical passages on marriage, I want to make a fundamental observation: the Bible is a big book, and it says relatively little about marriage. While there are important passages on marriage, and while the Bible does speak very highly of marriage, it's important that we understand the Bible is not *about* marriage.

Marriage is a minor theme in the Bible. And the major theme is God. On every page, the Bible is a book about God. His character, His world, His people, His promises, His future, His glory. Everything we say about marriage must first be seen in light of the Bible's emphasis on God. If we are going to view marriage accurately, we must view it in relation to God.

For the sake of your marriage, then, stop thinking about marriage for a moment. Think about God. That probably sounds odd, but it's important. Jesus didn't say a lot about marriage, but on a few occasions He mentioned marriage to keep us from over-exalting it. Did you catch that? Jesus, in a few different situations, pointed to marriage and told His audience *not to overvalue it.*

Consider, for example, Matthew 10. In this setting, Jesus was giving a job description to His disciples. He also prepared them for the persecution they were sure to encounter, and told them what following Him would mean for their family life:

> "I have come to set a man against his father, and a daughter against her mother, and a daughter-in-law against her mother-in-law. And a person's enemies will be those of his own household. Whoever loves father or mother more than me is not worthy of me, and whoever loves son or daughter more than me is not worthy of me. And whoever does not take his cross and follow me is not worthy of me. Whoever finds his life will lose it, and whoever loses his life for my sake will find it." (vv. 35–39)

Jesus didn't mention marriage here, but He was clear that the disciples' families could not take priority over the mission He was giving them. On another occasion, Jesus turned to the large crowds following Him and said:

> "If anyone comes to me and does not hate his own father and
> mother and wife and children and brothers and sisters, yes, and
> even his own life, he cannot be my disciple. Whoever does not
> bear his own cross and come after me cannot be my disciple."
> (Luke 14:26–27)

"Hate your own wife" is probably not the advice you were expecting to receive from a study on marriage. But that's how Jesus instructs the husbands who were interested in following Him. The point is the same in Luke 14 and Matthew 10—you can't follow Jesus if you're clinging too closely to your family. No relationship takes priority over your relationship with Jesus. You can't even cling to your own life. Following Jesus has to be more important than your family, than your marriage, even than your desire to live.

Jesus also taught that marriage is temporary. The Sadducees thought they could stump Jesus with a complex hypothetical situation. A woman's husband dies, so she marries his brother. Then he dies, so she marries the next brother. This continues until finally she finds herself married to the seventh brother. So, they ask Jesus, which brother will she be married to in the resurrection? The Sadducees did not believe in the resurrection of the dead, and they thought they were exposing the absurdity of believing in an afterlife.

Jesus escaped their supposed dilemma with ease:

> But Jesus answered them, "You are wrong, because you know
> neither the Scriptures nor the power of God. For in the resurrec-
> tion they neither marry nor are given in marriage, but are like
> angels in heaven." (Matthew 22:29–30)

What the Sadducees saw as a fundamental flaw in the logic of the resurrection, Jesus sidestepped by pointing out that we will not be married in the afterlife. That might sound disturbing, but we have to trust God's wisdom here. Whatever we will experience in the new heavens and new earth, it is guaranteed to be more amazing, more rich, than what we experience now. "Love never ends" (1 Cor. 13:8), but marriage is for this life only.

The point is, if we put all of our hopes and invest all of our resources into our marriages, then we are not investing in eternity. Jesus is pointing us to something that transcends marriage. Something greater. It is possible to overvalue marriage; we need to hear these strong words from Jesus lest we make our marriages into idols.

3. *Read Matthew 10:37, 22:30, and Luke 14:26. What do you think Jesus is getting at in these passages, and how should these bold statements affect the way we view our marriages?*

4. *We often have a tendency to take marriage—which is a very good thing—and make it into an ultimate thing. Have you seen this happen, either in your own marriage or someone else's? What does this look like when it happens?*

5. *Why do you think we tend to over-exalt marriage like this?*

6. *Why does it matter so much?*

We will not see marriage accurately until we see it in relation to God. And until we see God accurately, we have no hope for a healthy marriage. We cannot understand God's design for marriage until we get to know the God who designed it. Most of the problems we experience in marriage stem from a misunderstanding of God, from a lack of relationship with Him.

Most marriage problems are not really marriage problems; they're God problems. Maybe this sounds like an odd statement, or maybe it sounds obvious. Either way, if God is the one who created us—who designed us in every detail, both as a species and as individuals—then He understands how we work. He understands how our relationships with one another function best.

So if we misunderstand the God who made us, and if we fail to relate to Him properly, things are bound to go wrong. This is why Jesus insisted that the most important command is, "you shall love the Lord your God with all your heart and with all your soul and with all your mind and with all your strength" (Mark 12:30) and told us to "seek first the kingdom of God and his righteousness" (Matt. 6:33). This is why David passionately declared,

> *One thing* have I asked of the LORD,
>   that will I seek after:
> that I may dwell in the house of the LORD
>   all the days of my life,
> to gaze upon the beauty of the LORD
>   and to inquire in his temple.
>   (Psalm 27:4, emphasis added)

Maybe you've never considered your struggles in marriage in light of your relationship with God. If that's so, give it some thought. Use your imagination. How does your relationship with God affect your relationship with your spouse?

7. *How might most of our common marriage problems actually be problems in our relationships with God? Consider using examples or personal testimonies.*

We simply cannot function properly in this world without a proper view of God. We cannot function properly in marriage without a proper view of God. It's His world, and He has designed us to be dependent on Him, to desire Him, to pursue Him, to abide in Him. Jesus goes so far as to say, "apart from me you can do nothing" (John 15:5).

Because of this, we need to take time to either acquaint or reacquaint ourselves with God. This is not something that we can accomplish in an instant, nor is it a project we will ever complete. We always need to be drawing closer to God. But the best way to begin strengthening your marriage is to develop a pattern of pursuing God.

"The fear of the LORD is the beginning of wisdom, and the knowledge of the Holy One is insight" (Prov. 9:10). Knowing God means seeing Him in His glory. It means developing a high view of God, an appropriate fear of God. Take some time to assess your holy respect for your Creator.

8. *In the two columns below, identify the ways that you do and don't fear God. This may be tricky, because most of us are quick to affirm that we fear God. But try to honestly weigh your heart and actions. What actions demonstrate that you do or don't fear God? Once you have made some notes, share your thoughts with your spouse or with the group, giving them a chance to relate, challenge, or encourage you.*

WAYS I FEAR GOD	WAYS I DON'T FEAR GOD

9.   *What would it look like to deepen your relationship with God? There are many trite, cheesy, and oversimplified ways to answer this question, but try to be practical, honest, and passionate as you answer. God made you, He loves you, and He wants to know and be known by you. How can you make progress in this?*

10. *When you think about your marriage (or the marriage you may one day have), how do you think a closer relationship with God will actually affect your relationship with your spouse?*

11. *How can you build this prioritizing of your relationship with God into your marriage? It's easy to say "Yeah, I'll work on that," but you need to work together with your spouse to ensure that this is a continual part of your relationship with one another. How can you help each other pursue God every day of your lives?*

God is the point of your marriage. You must reflect Him. Your marriage must reflect Him. Most of our troubles in marriage are about the satisfaction we're not receiving, the frustration we're experiencing, the misunderstanding we're having to endure. But if marriage is about God, then these issues fade into the background. So here is the real question: Is *God* receiving satisfaction through your marriage? Is *God* frustrated with the way you are living with your spouse? Is *God* being misunderstood in your marriage?

These are the *true* marriage problems. But only if you reclaim the *true* point of marriage. If you hold on to the traditional wisdom about marriage and pursue a healthy marriage for the sake of your own happiness, you will be missing the very reason for which God created marriage. Don't waste your marriage on your own happiness. See marriage as the gift it is. See marriage in light of God's purpose.

12. *Spend some time in prayer. Ask God to reveal those areas in your understanding of marriage that do not line up with His purpose for marriage. Ask Him to give you a greater picture of Himself. Pray that He would continually draw you and your spouse closer to Himself, and that your pursuit of Him would be the true priority in your marriage.*

REFLECTIONS ON...

Marriage Isn't that Great

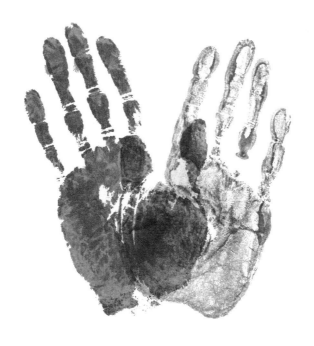

SESSION TWO

Pursue the Perfect Marriage

For more information on the material in this session,
read Chapter 2 of the book *You & Me Forever*
and take a few minutes to watch the relevant
video(s) at youandmeforever.org.

Consider two different approaches to marriage. On the one hand, many people work on their marriages so that they look good. No one wants to be that couple that is always fighting, always at odds, always unhappy. Everyone wants to have the kind of marriage their friends and family admire. So many couples put time and energy into their marriages in order to create the perfect family life and make themselves look good.

The other approach to marriage is intent on making God look good. These couples see marriage as a reflection of God, so they work hard on their marriages. They confess their sins, humble themselves, serve one another, and do everything they can to display God's love in their marriage. This approach to marriage is rewarding, but it is not self-focused. It's not about how other people perceive your marriage. It's not about making yourselves look or feel good. Couples that take this approach to marriage are captivated with God's glory, and their marriages are focused on showing the world who

God is. The great part is that those who focus on God's glory end up with a marriage that others admire!

In the Bible's longest passage on marriage, Ephesians 5:22–33, Paul takes the focus off of our earthly marriages and points our attention toward the perfect marriage: the marriage between Jesus Christ and the church. So as you continue to think through your own marriage and how it can best glorify God, it is essential that you follow Paul's lead and think deeply about the way Jesus relates to us as His church. In an effort to be a better husband or wife, then, consider what God has done for you through Jesus Christ.

1. *Read Ephesians 5:22–33. How does God describe His relationship with the church here?*

2. *How does this description affect your view of God, and how should it affect your relationship with Him?*

Having a good relationship with your spouse requires that you first have a good relationship with God. There is no way to be a Christ-like spouse apart from drawing closer to Christ. Unfortunately, many Christians assume that attending church services or saying a prayer is enough. It doesn't matter how powerful a religious experience you've had, how long you've been a Christian, or how faithful a churchgoer you have been. If you are not growing in your relationship with Jesus, if you are not actively pursuing Him, then you are disconnecting yourself from the source of life. Jesus was clear: "apart from me you can do nothing" (John 15:5). Yet so many Christians assume that they can be the kind of spouse God wants them to be even as they neglect their relationship with Jesus.

Whether you have been a Christian for decades or this is an entirely new concept for you, it's essential that you take time to consider where you stand with God. Honestly assess your heart here. Don't settle for quick answers like, "Yes, I believe the gospel." It may be that you discover that you don't really know God yet. If so, this could be the greatest week of your life! Be honest with your spouse or group about it, and make this the week you turn to Jesus. Don't ever take this lightly. It's the difference between life and death, heaven and hell. Take this opportunity to consider what it is that Jesus has done for you and how these realities should affect your life and marriage. We will continue to explore marriage in greater depth, but the way forward in your marriage is a deepening of your relationship with God.

3. *Consider the good news of what Jesus has done and how these realities should affect you. In the left hand column, list some of the things that Jesus has done for you (forgiven your sin, died in your place, etc.). In the right hand column, list some of the ways that these realities should transform your life and your marriage. The right hand column will require some thought and imagination, but it's important, so take your time. Once you've filled in these columns, share some of your thoughts with your spouse and/or your group.*

WHAT JESUS HAS DONE	HOW THIS SHOULD TRANSFORM MY LIFE & MARRIAGE

4. *Do you need to get right with God in some respect? Take some time right now to do that. In light of who Jesus is and what He has done, what do you need to say to Him? What do you need to confess? What do you need to believe and embrace and put into practice? Don't move on until you've done this. Consider sharing some of your thoughts with your spouse and/or your group.*

We often identify the good things we ought to be doing, but then fail to live them out. Paul describes this frustrating process in Romans 7: "I do not understand my own actions. For I do not do what I want, but I do the very thing I hate" (v. 15). Paul is depicting a person trying to pursue godliness apart from the power of God's Spirit.

The Holy Spirit changes everything. How many couples have seen the dysfunction in their marriages and decided to work harder to make the needed changes? And yet the Bible promises us that apart from the Spirit, our intense labor will be fruitless. God gave us the Holy Spirit so that every aspect of our lives would be transformed. He lives within us, changing us from the inside out.

> If the Spirit of him who raised Jesus from the dead dwells in
> you, he who raised Christ Jesus from the dead will also give life
> to your mortal bodies through his Spirit who dwells in you.
> (Romans 8:11)

This is the difference between being dead and being alive. The Bible gives some powerful images of what it looks like to be made alive in Christ through the power of the Spirit. Consider some of these images and make some notes about how this life-giving power should begin to transform your life and your marriage.

5. *Read Ezekiel 36:25–27 and 37:1–14. What strikes you in these passages? What do you find interesting or challenging?*

6. *Now think practically about Ezekiel's prophecy and vision. This is supposed to be reality for those who follow Jesus. How is the new life provided through the Spirit of God actually shaping your life today? How about your marriage?*

Now take a few minutes to read Romans 8:1–17. This New Testament passage further explores the reality promised in Ezekiel 36 and 37. These passages are all about moving from death to life, about God taking a lifeless, unresponsive heart and recreating it into something new and living. Consider how the powerful truths of Romans 8 should be shaping your life. Examine your marriage in light of Paul's words.

7. *What aspects of your marriage make sense in light of the Spirit's life-giving power? What aspects of your marriage don't make sense in light of the Spirit?*

ASPECTS OF MY MARRIAGE THAT MAKE SENSE IN LIGHT OF THE SPIRIT	ASPECTS OF MY MARRIAGE THAT DON'T MAKE SENSE IN LIGHT OF THE SPIRIT

8. *If the Spirit is truly inside of you—if you have access to the same power that raised Jesus from the grave—how should the elements in the right hand column begin to change? What can you be doing to work to this end?*

One battle we will constantly face as we seek to shift from a self-focused marriage to a God-focused marriage is with our own feelings. Feelings are deep-seated in our lives and in our marriages. If your spouse lies to you, it makes sense that you would not feel like forgiving him or her. If your spouse has anger issues, it makes sense that you would feel anger in return.

God knows you have these feelings, yet He calls you to obey anyways. God's commands do not wait for our feelings. Jesus begged God to let the bitter cup of His crucifixion pass. He didn't "feel like" enduring an unjust trial and excruciating death. But praise God that Jesus' feelings did not have the final say. Instead, He chose to pray, "Not my will, but yours, be done" (Luke 22:42).

Imitating Christ in our marriages will mean putting our feelings into perspective. It's right to feel; it's unbiblical to make our decisions solely on the basis of what we feel like doing. As you examine your marriage and consider what it will take to be Christ-like in your marriage, take stock of what this battle with your feelings will entail. Make some notes below.

9. *What feelings do you need to let go of as you pursue Christ-likeness in your marriage? Why?*

10. *How can you begin to do this? Practically speaking, what will it look like to respond to your feelings with biblical truth? Do you have any examples?*

Perhaps the biggest obstacle you will have to overcome in your desire to glorify God in your marriage is your past failure. If you're living in a difficult marriage, you've probably tried to turn things around in the past, and you've probably failed to achieve the results you wanted. You probably see your weakness, your inability to produce change, and it probably makes you nervous about putting more effort into your marriage.

But Paul tells us that we can actually rejoice *in our weakness*, because God's strength is clearly displayed in our weakness.

> He said to me, "My grace is sufficient for you, for my power is made perfect in weakness." Therefore I will boast all the more gladly of my weaknesses, so that the power of Christ may rest upon me. For the sake of Christ, then, I am content with weaknesses, insults, hardships, persecutions, and calamities. For when I am weak, then I am strong. (2 Corinthians 12:9–10)

You may think the struggle and inadequacy you are experiencing should excuse your ungodly thoughts and actions in your marriage. Yet Paul says that this is exactly when God empowers us. Every time we find ourselves feeling powerless we should be reminded that our strength comes from God. When you are weak, you are strong, because God's grace is sufficient.

11. Based on 2 Corinthians 12:1–10, how can your weakness in marriage reveal God to the world? Why do you think God chooses to do it this way?

12. *Spend some time in prayer. Ask God to reach into your heart and expose your motivations. Offer your marriage and your dreams for marriage to Him as a tool for glorifying Himself. Ask Him to make you Christ-like as a spouse, and pray that He would empower you in the midst of your weakness.*

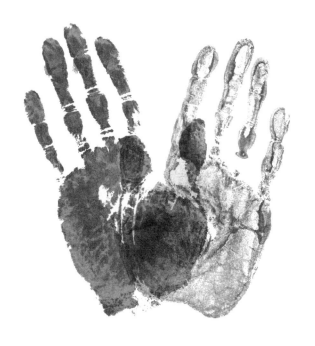

SESSION THREE

Learn to Fight Well

For more information on the material in this session,
read Chapter 3 of the book *You & Me Forever*
and take a few minutes to watch the relevant
video(s) at youandmeforever.org.

As we saw in the previous session, Paul makes the startling statement that husbands should love their wives *as Christ loved the church.* In saying this, Paul uses Jesus as the model for our marriages. This shouldn't be too surprising. After all, being a Christian means being a follower of Jesus, and following Jesus means imitating Him in all aspects of our lives. As Paul said, "Be imitators of me as I am of Christ" (1 Cor. 11:1).

Imagine being married to Jesus. How sacrificial would He be in meeting your needs? How clear would He be in showing His love? What sin could you begin to display without Him lovingly calling you back to godliness? What offense would He not quickly forgive? If we took the biblical call to follow Jesus seriously, then we would begin to look like Jesus in the midst of our marriages. So as you continue to examine your marriage, take some time to think about Jesus and consider what it means to imitate Him.

1. *What makes Jesus compelling and beautiful? Don't answer this quickly. What aspects of Jesus' character draw you to Him? What actions did He perform that fascinate you? Share these with your spouse and/or your group.*

2. *As much as we are inspired by the picture of Jesus we see in the gospels, it's not always easy to imagine what being like Jesus would look like in our modern context. Spend a few minutes discussing this. If you were to live like Jesus today, what would this look like in the context of your daily life?*

Everything that Jesus said and did is worthy of admiration and imitation. It would be healthy for all of us to work through a list of Jesus' attributes and consider how each aspect of His character should shape us as we relate to our spouses. That would make an excellent life-long project. But for the sake of this study, consider just one attribute of Jesus: His humility.

Philippians 2 is a striking passage. Paul tells the Christians in Philippi that they should be humbly looking out not only for their own interests, but also for the interests of others. And the example he uses of humility at first seems illogical. Paul points to Jesus (whom Paul says was "in the form of God" and "equal with God") as the prime example of humility. The one Being who has no deficiency, no need, no imperfection, and no reason to be ashamed is Paul's example of what humility looks like.

Take a minute to read Philippians 2:1–11. As you read this description of Jesus' self-emptying humility, consider how Christ-likeness in this area would transform your life and your marriage.

3. *What strikes you about Jesus' example of humility as described in Philippians 2:5–11?*

4. *If you were to imitate Jesus' example of humility in your marriage, how would your relationship with your spouse be transformed? (Think practically here. Don't settle for answers like "It would be better." Consider some of the things you would be doing differently, along with which aspects of your marriage would be changed and how.)*

The opposite of humility is pride, and unfortunately, pride shows up in everything we do. Pride is deadly to marriage because it takes a relationship between two people and attempts to focus it on only one person. When you find yourself desperate to win an argument, when you insist on casting the blame on your spouse, or when you allow yourself to be served more often than you serve, you are exhibiting the opposite of humility. While it might make you feel better in the short term, pride is guaranteed to ruin your marriage.

But the worst aspect of pride is this: "God opposes the proud, but gives grace to the humble." (James 4:6) There are so many reasons to rid ourselves of pride and pursue humility, but none can compare with this. When we are prideful, God is actively opposing us. I can't think of anything more terrifying. We are utterly dependent on God's grace as we try to imitate Jesus in marriage. So anytime we identify even a trace of pride in the way we are relating to our spouses, we need to immediately confess that pride and beg God to grant us humble hearts.

5. *How do you see pride show up in your relationship with your spouse? Give some examples.*

Jesus actually calls us to go deeper than eliminating prideful thoughts. The call to follow Jesus is actually a call to die:

> Then Jesus told his disciples, "If anyone would come after me, let him deny himself and take up his cross and follow me. For whoever would save his life will lose it, but whoever loses his life for my sake will find it." (Matthew 16:24–25).

> I have been crucified with Christ. It is no longer I who live, but Christ lives in me. (Galatians 2:20)

This language of self-denial, of taking up your cross and giving up your life, describes the essence of following Jesus. As popular as it may be to assume that we can "follow Jesus" without adjusting our lifestyle, Jesus calls us to lay our lives down and to pursue Him rather than our own agenda. As you think through pride and humility in the context of marriage, consider how Jesus' language of dying to self should affect your life in general, and your marriage in particular.

6. *What would it look like to die to yourself? Don't settle for vague answers like "I'd have to give up my desires." Get practical. What pursuits, actions, or emotions would you need to let go of? What would those pursuits, actions, or emotions need to be replaced with?*

7. *Think specifically of your marriage relationship. What would it look like to die to yourself in the context of your marriage?*

In the previous session, you looked briefly at Ephesians 5:22–33 and considered the implications of this passage for the way we view our relationship with God. In this session, you will look at the passage again, this time focusing on Paul's instructions for the way husbands should relate to their wives, and vice versa.

Take a minute to read carefully through Ephesians 5:22–33 (even if you read it carefully in the previous session). Use the questions below to help you process the material, but be sure to share with your spouse and/or your group about any statements or features in this passage that stand out to you, even if it's not addressed in one of these study questions.

8.   What stands out to you about the instructions that Paul gives to wives?

9.   What stands out to you about the instructions that Paul gives to husbands?

10. Jesus "gave himself" for the church (v. 25). The necessary self-sacrifice in marriage means that your relationship with your spouse will at times be painful. Based on either your experience or your expectations (if you're not currently married), how does loving sacrificially cause pain? Do you have any examples of this?

11. Submission is a tricky topic to discuss, and it grates against our sensibilities. But Christ-like humility puts submission in perspective. How should Jesus' example of humility affect the way you view Paul's call for wives to submit to their husbands?

If marriage were about our own happiness, then we would need to throw out much of what Paul says in Ephesians 5. But because the model for marriage is Christ's relationship with his church—since we are called to imitate Christ's sacrificial love for the church—our view of marriage must go much deeper than our own pursuit of happiness. Marriage is about God's glory. It's about the profound mystery of the God who humbled Himself, took on the form of a servant, and sacrificed Himself for the sake of those He loves.

Paul says in Romans 12:10 that we are to "outdo one another in showing honor." Can you imagine if this became an accurate description of your marriage? What problems would you face if you were both primarily concerned with honoring each other, rather than exalting yourselves? If you took this self-sacrificing love as seriously as Jesus did, then your spouse would have no grounds for complaining, and you wouldn't respond in anger even if he or she did.

Once again, marriage is about God's glory. It's about His mission for us. Only those marriages that are characterized by humility call attention to the self-sacrificing love of Jesus. Until every ounce of pride is drained from your marriage, you will be misunderstanding and misusing marriage. What you need more than anything else for your marriage is God's grace, and James is clear that God's grace comes to those who pursue humility.

12. *Spend some time in prayer. Ask God to help you identify your pride and to replace it with humility. Pray that your marriage would be characterized by humility and self-sacrificing love.*

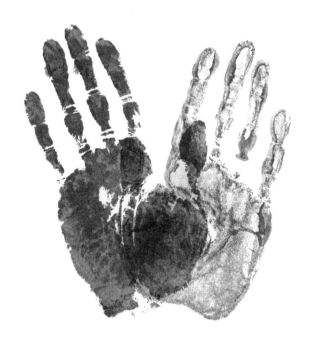

SESSION FOUR

Don't Waste Your Marriage

For more information on the material in this session,
read Chapter 4 of the book *You & Me Forever*
and take a few minutes to watch the relevant
video(s) at youandmeforever.org.

Judging by the actions of the majority of Christian couples, we seem to have made happy families our mission. What is your mission? What does your family spend time doing? What concerns are most important? What would you identify as your biggest problems or your most significant goals?

If you are a typical couple, a large portion of your time and energy goes into building and maintaining a happy family. And we should be investing in our marriages. But families are not the goal. Happiness is not the mission. Something far greater is at stake.

Jesus' mission was discipleship. From the very beginning, Jesus was making disciples—leading them, teaching them, and sending them out. When He first called Peter and Andrew, they were fishing. Jesus approached them and said, "Follow me, and I will make you fishers of men" (Matt. 4:19). The disciples followed Jesus for three years, then He sent them out with these simple words: "Make disciples."

"All authority in heaven and on earth has been given to me. Go therefore and make disciples of all nations, baptizing them in the name of the Father and of the Son and of the Holy Spirit, teaching them to observe all that I have commanded you. And behold, I am with you always, to the end of the age." (Matthew 28:18–20)

That was the mission Jesus gave His original disciples, and it has been the mission of the church ever since. It remains our mission today.

Many Christians separate their lives into tidy compartments: work, spouse, kids, friends, church, etc. So we might be tempted to see these pursuits as separate tasks we have to fit in: I need to be making disciples, I need to work on my marriage, I need to pray. But that's not how it works. Making disciples is not a compartment of your spiritual life. Making disciples is the mission. So every ounce of time and energy you have needs to be directed toward that goal. That means your marriage is not an end in itself, your marriage is one important area in which you need to pursue the mission of making disciples. This will mean husbands and wives pushing one another to become better followers of Jesus, but it will also mean working side by side in an effort to make disciples. Take some time to consider how this simple command should shape your marriage.

1. *Would you say your marriage is oriented toward making disciples? How so? If not, what do you think this might look like?*

As we lose sight of our God-given mission, we also tend to forget that we are living in a battle. Many Christians appear to be entirely unaware of the true struggle that takes place all around them. Biblically speaking, there is an actual battle raging at every moment.

Read the following passages slowly:

- *2 Corinthians 10:3–6*
- *Ephesians 6:10–20*
- *2 Timothy 2:1–7*

Think deeply about what Paul says in these verses. Meditate on the truth that the battle Paul describes in these passages is going on *right here, right now, as you read and discuss.* After you've spent some time meditating on these passages, write down some of your thoughts below.

2. *How would you describe the battle that is taking place around you at every moment?*

3. *To what extent would you say that you act as though you are naively unaware of the real battle going on? Why do you say that?*

As Christian couples tiptoe through life, seeking fleeting forms of happiness, pursuing unattainable standards of "success," and trying to build happy families, the real battle continues. The longer we remain fixated on our own pursuits, the more we squander time and energy that could be devoted to God's mission.

You might think that unless you devote every ounce of your strength and every free moment to strengthening your marriage, the whole thing will fall apart. Marriage is difficult, and it does require work. Perhaps yours is barely holding together or you're afraid of what might happen if you took your eyes off your marriage and turned your attention elsewhere.

But marriage was not designed to be the focus of our lives. If all of our attention stays there, then we are actually misusing marriage. It's possible to focus on your marriage so much that it falls apart. Marriage was designed to function in the context of God's mission. If each partner is not pursuing God's calling, then the marriage is headed for trouble. For the sake of your marriage, then, put your focus back on the mission God has given you. When we work side by side for God's glory, our marriages fall into place—we form a bond with each other naturally. When we put all of our effort into building stronger marriages, our energy is wasted and our marriages are threatened.

Paul's desire for the Philippians was that together they would be "standing firm in one spirit, with one mind striving side by side for the faith of the gospel" (Phil. 1:27). That was his prayer for the church, but it also provides a good model for marriage. If your marriage is going to be shaped by God's mission, it will mean looking outward, with each of you laboring side by side for the sake of the gospel. What are you doing to serve the people around you? It's amazing to see problems miraculously shrink as you look outside of yourself and begin to help other people with their needs.

4. *Explain this concept more fully. How should fighting side by side in pursuit of the mission that God has given us lead to a healthier marriage?*

5. *What steps can you begin taking right now to make this kind of co-laboring in pursuit of God's mission a reality in your marriage? What is keeping you from this and how can you overcome these obstacles?*

One of the most amazing statements in the Great Commission is Jesus' promise that as we go out and make disciples, "I am with you always, to the end of the age" (Matt. 28:20). Jesus sends us out, but He promises to be with us. This means that if we are pursuing His mission, we will experience His presence. If we are not pursuing the mission, His presence in not guaranteed in the same sense.

This is yet another reason to pursue the mission that Jesus left for us. If we want to experience God in the midst of our marriages, then our marriages need to be shaped by the mission. If our marriages are focused on making disciples, then Jesus will be with us always. There is nothing like serving alongside your spouse and knowing that God is with you, blessing your efforts.

6. *Have you had times in your life and/or your marriage where you were pursuing God's mission and experienced His presence in a unique way? How so? If you have not yet experienced God's presence in the midst of serving, what do you think it might look like?*

7. *Where could you and your spouse begin serving that would put you in the line of God's presence and blessing?*

While God designed marriage to function properly as we pursue His mission, many Christian marriages lose sight of God's mission because they get overly focused on their own marriages. Paul warned against this:

> I want you to be free from anxieties. The unmarried man is anxious about the things of the Lord, how to please the Lord. But the married man is anxious about worldly things, how to please his wife, and his interests are divided…I say this for your own benefit, not to lay any restraint upon you, but to promote good order and to secure your undivided devotion to the Lord. (1 Corinthians 7:32–35)

This passage challenges many of our assumptions about marriage. Paul even goes so far as to say, "let those who have wives live as though they had none" (v. 29). The Christians in Corinth had written to Paul, asking him to clarify some questions about engagement and marriage (see verses 1 and 25). Paul's answer reveals that there is something greater at stake than the concerns of marriage. If you're unmarried, consider your singleness an opportunity to serve God with greater freedom. If you're married, be sure that your marriage is focused on pleasing the Lord and is not weakening your devotion to Him. If you're engaged ("betrothed"), don't simply pursue the option that will make you happiest, ask which option will make you most effective for God's mission.

8. *Read through 1 Corinthians 7 (especially verses 25–35). What are the main points Paul is making here? How would you summarize Paul's overall point?*

9. *What are some ways that marriage can lead us away from an undivided devotion to the Lord?*

10. *What would it look like if you took Paul's teaching here seriously? In other words, if you took Paul's concerns about devotion to the Lord and applied them to your marriage, how would your relationship with your spouse look different than it does right now? If you are unmarried, how should this passage affect your thoughts about and/or pursuit of marriage?*

Getting on track with God's mission does not happen automatically. It certainly requires more than a one-time decision. That's why Paul said, "I discipline my body and keep it under control" (1 Cor. 9:27) and challenged Timothy to train himself for godliness

(1 Tim. 4:7). You must make a decision to pursue the mission of making disciples, but it also requires continuous training. Just as an athlete trains for victory, so we must devote ourselves to our God-given task.

Hebrews picks up this athlete imagery and calls us to "lay aside every weight, and sin which clings so closely, and…run with endurance the race that is set before us" (Heb. 12:1). One of the most difficult aspects of training is letting go of everything that would slow us down. Obviously this will include "the sin which clings so closely," but it will also mean letting go of good things that distract us from what is best. Take these calls seriously and consider what it will take to shape your life around God's mission.

11. *What would it look like (both individually and as a couple) to begin training yourself for the mission?*

12. *What is hindering you and your spouse from running hard after Christ and pursuing the mission (sin, bitterness, resentment, continued struggles, etc.)? Be as open as possible. Be prepared for this to expose a number of issues that may be difficult to resolve. It's worth it. Your relationship is worth it. God's mission is certainly worth it.*

13. *Spend some time in prayer. Ask God to give you a passion for His mission of making disciples. Pray for unity as you and your spouse seek to pursue this mission together. Ask God to shape every area of your life around His glory and His mission.*

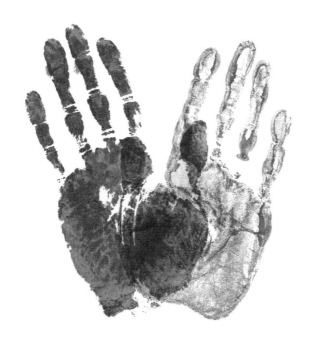

SESSION FIVE

Is there Hope for Us?

For more information on the material in this session,
read Chapter 5 of the book *You & Me Forever*
and take a few minutes to watch the relevant
video(s) at youandmeforever.org.

Make no mistake: the day is coming when you and your family will stand face to face with God. Depending on where your relationship with God stands, that's either an unbelievably terrifying or unimaginably wonderful thought. This is where your life is headed; it's where all of history culminates.

If we could only take stock of how we would feel at that moment—what we would find important, what we would regret, what we would be grateful to have pursued—our lives would be changed forever. I can't imagine John coming "back to earth" after the vision he received in Revelation and continuing on as though nothing had happened.

We often start with our own dreams for our families and then build our marriages from there. What if we started with a vision of the end and worked backwards, building the kind of marriage that will prepare us to stand before God? As distant as that day may seem, this encounter with God is a certainty—it is more real than any ideal for marriage you could come up with on your own.

1. *Picture standing with your family before God at the end of your life. If your marriage continues on just as it is, what do you think you will regret when you look back on your marriage that day? What would it look like to begin weeding out these elements now?*

2. *What practices or characteristics in your marriage do you think you will be pleased with when you reach that day? How can you continue to cultivate and build upon these elements?*

The Bible calls our attention to this encounter with God often. One way that the Bible does this is by speaking of the rewards available to us in heaven. While some Christians are uncomfortable with the concept of seeking rewards, Jesus actually commanded us to pursue them.

> "Do not lay up for yourselves treasures on earth, where moth and rust destroy and where thieves break in and steal, but lay up for yourselves treasures in heaven, where neither moth nor rust destroys and where thieves do not break in and steal. For where your treasure is, there your heart will be also." (Matthew 6:19–21)

God promises to reward us in heaven for pursuing Him in this life. He gives us a vision of the end and calls us to shape our present in light of that future. Take a few minutes to consider this deeply.

3. *Read the following passages. (If you don't want to spend the time reading through all of the passages now, choose a few to look up.) After you've read and considered what these passages say about eternal rewards, make a few notes and share your thoughts with your spouse and/or your group. What rewards are promised? How are these rewards attained?*

1 Corinthians 3:10–15

2 Corinthians 4:17–18

Mark 9:38–50

Mark 10:28–30

Matthew 5:1–12

Matthew 6:1-8

Matthew 6:16–21

Matthew 10:40-42

Luke 6:20–36

Colossians 3:23–25

Revelation 11:16–18

We need to know these promises. But we also need to believe them: "without faith it is impossible to please him, for whoever would draw near to God must believe that he exists and that he rewards those who seek him" (Heb. 11:6). Knowing that God promises these things is not enough. We must believe them so fully act on them so aggressively that our lives would be seen as tragedies if they proved to be false promises. Has your marriage been shaped by God's promises regarding the future? How would you know if it has? Consider what your marriage would look like if you gave no thought to God's promises compared to what it would look like if you fully believed these promises.

4. *In the columns below, describe the ideal marriage in two very different scenarios. In the left hand column, imagine that there is no God, no mission, and no eternal rewards, then write down what an ideal marriage would look like in*

that context. What would your goals be? What would you want to get out of this type of marriage? In the right hand column, imagine the God of the Bible and the promises He offers, then write down what an ideal marriage would look like in that context.

AN IDEAL MARRIAGE WITHOUT THE PROMISE OF ETERNAL REWARDS	AN IDEAL MARRIAGE IN LIGHT OF THE PROMISE OF ETERNAL REWARDS

5. *Which column best reflects your marriage? Why do you say that?*

One measure of your longing for God is what you would give up in order to be with Him. Most Christians are quick to say that they'd give up anything to be with Jesus. But how many of us have thought through the implications of this kind of statement? In my experience, most Christians would quickly choose to stay with their families rather than going to be with Jesus. This reveals two huge problems. First, it shows that the family has become an idol. Anything we are not willing to part with for God's sake is an idol—it has replaced God in our lives. And second, this shows that we do not truly believe God's promises. If we really believed the Bible's descriptions of Jesus and of our glorious future with Him, then we wouldn't hesitate to join Him at the earliest opportunity. As Paul said, "My desire is to depart and be with Christ, for that is far better" (Philip. 1:23).

6. *If you were given the choice today between staying with your family longer and going immediately to be with Jesus, which would you choose? Don't just give the church answer, try to be completely honest. What would make this decision difficult? Which factors push you one way or the other? What do you think your honest answer reveals about your heart?*

If you are hesitant to affirm that you would choose to be with Jesus immediately, it's likely that your spouse is serving as a replacement for God in some sense. This is common, even in Christian marriages. We look to our spouses for validation, identity, reassurance, and love. Of course, God designed marriage as a means of meeting many of our needs. But ultimately, everything we need comes from God. He often chooses to use our spouses in meeting our needs, but if my hope or identity becomes rooted more in my spouse than in God, then my spouse has become an idol, and I am not relating to God properly.

You will probably be quick to deny that your spouse functions as an idol in your life, but I'm asking you to take some time to consider this possibility. Think about the way you view your spouse, the way you relate to one another, and how all of this ties in with your relationship with God.

7. *Generally speaking, what things do we try to get from our spouses that we should be getting from God? Specifically, what are you trying to get from your spouse that should ultimately come from God?*

8. *What would it look like to expect and receive these things from God?*

Living in light of God's promises means embracing them deeply. It means more than memorizing verses (though this can be hugely beneficial)—we need to be meditating on God's truth, letting it sink deeply into our souls, and shaping our lives with the characteristics that make us into the people God calls us to be. Paul uses an agricultural metaphor and refers to this process as "sowing to the Spirit."

9. *Read Galatians 6:7–10. What would you say you have been "sowing" into your life and your marriage? What have you been "reaping" as a result?*

10. *As a couple, what would it look like to "sow to the Spirit" in your marriage? Think very practically here. Avoid simple answers like "we need to love each other more." Try to paint a picture that includes your daily activities and factors in your personalities, life situations, etc.*

The best way to conclude this session is by carefully reading God's brilliant vision for the end and allowing that vision to sink in deeply. As you read the last two chapters of the Bible, try to immerse yourself in the scene. See what John sees, hear what he hears, feel what he must have felt. Let these images form your imagination and direct your heart. After reading carefully and meditating, make some notes below.

11. *Read Revelation 21–22. What stands out in this passage? What longings does this description of the new heavens and new earth satisfy? What passions does it kindle? How should this powerful image shape your marriage today?*

12. *Spend some time in prayer. Ask God to shape your heart and imagination with His promises. Pray for faith to cling to these and ask Him to empower you as you seek to shape your life in light of eternity.*

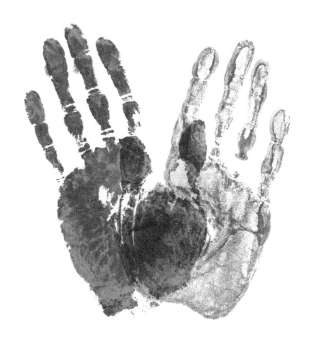

SESSION SIX

What's Really Best for the Kids?

For more information on the material in this session,
read Chapter 6 of the book *You & Me Forever*
and take a few minutes to watch the relevant video(s)
at youandmeforever.org. You will discuss elements
of Chapter 6 in the next session as well, so if some
point in the book does not come out in this week's
discussion, it will likely be covered in the next.

Most of us could never be accused of taking our responsibility as parents too lightly. We care deeply about our children, and we see our God-given task of raising them as a serious calling. Yet being serious is not enough. As we have seen, we can be serious about our marriages even as we take them in the wrong directions and distort them for the wrong purposes. The same is true of parenting. We can love our children immeasurably even as we lead them—with the best of intentions—away from God.

For many couples, much of their time as a married couple is devoted to parenting. So we will take this session and the next to explore what it means to raise children to

God's glory. Parenting is incredibly complex and difficult, and there is much to talk about. We will hardly scratch the surface in these two sessions, but our desire is to guide you in thinking about the overall goal and direction of your parenting.

1. *If you have children, briefly share your experience. What are your favorite aspects of parenting? What are the greatest difficulties? If you do not have children but would like to in the future, share your hopes and fears for parenting.*

One of the biggest indicators that parenting has gotten off track in our society is a host of grown children who don't know how to care for themselves or others. A childhood of constant pampering and being the center of attention creates adults who expect to be catered to, who see themselves as the center of the universe.

When parents serve their kids, their hearts are often pure. After all, God placed these children in your care, He wants you to provide for them and enable them to thrive. However, doing everything for our children teaches them that they are the most important thing in the world and it leaves them lacking in critical life skills. This approach can also reveal that our kids have become idols—that our kids are the most important part of our lives. If we parent as though our kids matter more than anything, we shouldn't be surprised when our kids start believing it. Teaching our children responsibility, service, and selflessness is vital to raising kids who will pursue God and His mission.

2. *Have you seen this shift from raising kids to be fully functioning adults to sim-*
    ply doing everything for them, either in your own parenting or in our society?
    Describe what each of these family dynamics looks like.

3. *What would you say is the appropriate balance between caring for your chil-*
    dren and teaching them to be responsible?

Many parents today simply want to be friends with their kids. And that's a beautiful
thing. Lisa and I have rich friendships with each of our children. However, we must
keep two things in mind. First, our culture has a weak view of friendship. Friends
are there to make you happy and to keep things fun. Friends would never call you
out on destructive behavior or hold you accountable for your actions. But the biblical
concept of friendship involves sharpening, shaping, hard words, and unconditional
love. Consider these proverbs:

> Iron sharpens iron,
>> and one man sharpens another. (Proverbs 27:17)

> Faithful are the wounds of a friend;
>> profuse are the kisses of an enemy. (Proverbs 27:6)

Our definition of a friend (someone who always keeps things fun and positive) actually better fits Proverbs' definition of an enemy. A friend is one who sharpens us, who wounds us in all of the right ways in order to make us better people. If we were friends to our kids in this sense, our relationships would be rich. As parents, we will have to do and say things that may make our kids dislike us for a time. But we can't let popularity outweigh the role God has given us in the lives of our children.

The other thing we need to keep in mind here is that God has placed you in your child's life *as a parent*. I know that's obvious, but it means that you have a God-given responsibility to discipline your children, to speak truth into their lives, and to acquaint them with the harder aspects of reality. Failing at these responsibilities in the name of "friendship" is poor parenting.

4. *What is the appropriate approach to being "friends" with your kids? How have you seen this go wrong (either in your own parenting or in society)? What are the consequences of swinging the pendulum too far in either direction?*

5. *Answer this question honestly: What would break your heart more? If your kids don't end up loving you? Or if they don't end up loving Jesus? Why do you say that? Be open here, this is an important question to consider and discuss.*

As a pastor for many years, I have seen many parents blame the church for their children's lack of love for God. Too many parents are counting on teachers and youth pastors to train their kids appropriately. While raising children should involve a supportive community, God calls us to be teaching our own children constantly:

> "Hear, O Israel: The LORD our God, the LORD is one. You shall love the LORD your God with all your heart and with all your soul and with all your might. And these words that I command you today shall be on your heart. *You shall teach them diligently to your children, and shall talk of them when you sit in your house, and when you walk by the way, and when you lie down, and when you rise.* You shall bind them as a sign on your hand, and they shall be as frontlets between your eyes. You shall write them on the doorposts of your house and on your gates." (Deuteronomy 6:4–8, emphasis added)

Our children will learn much from the other people that God brings into their lives, but we are not fulfilling our role as parents if we are not constantly teaching our kids. This will mean having direct conversations with them about God, His world, and His truth. Your children need to know that God is the most important thing in life. They need to know that His will matters most, that He is worth sacrificing for, that He loves them unconditionally, that His promises can be trusted, and a thousand other essential truths.

But teaching our kids means more than speaking truth into their lives. They also need to see that truth *demonstrated, played out* in your daily activities. If you teach your children that God's promises are trustworthy, but live as though they are not, what do you think they will end up believing? If you tell you kids that God is worth sacrificing for, yet you never make any sacrifices for His sake, how do you think they will respond?

The frightening truth is that we could say all of the right things to our children and yet renounce all of it with our lifestyles. A preacher can speak truth in a Sunday morning service that he doesn't apply to his own life. Some people will notice the inconsistency; many will not. But when it comes to our own children, they are with us all the time. They know what we value, how we spend our time, what motivates us. When we tell our children that God matters more than anything else, they will know the extent to which we actually believe that statement.

One of the greatest and most terrifying aspects of parenting is the opportunity to teach our kids the gospel. We should be doing this regularly, using every opportunity to speak about Jesus and what He has done. But we will also need to reinforce this teaching in the way we live and the way we parent. In my experience, very few Christians have taken the time to consider how the gospel should affect their daily lives. How should God's unmerited grace be modeled in the way I speak to my children? How should Jesus' humble service shape my interactions with my coworkers?

Unless we think through these concepts deeply, our children will grow up believing that the gospel is something we talk about, rather than something we live. Use the next several questions to evaluate your parenting and challenge your own heart. When you find an area that needs work, use it as an opportunity to question yourself. For example, if you are not displaying the gospel to your children, ask yourself if you truly understand and believe what God has done for you. Many of these are deep questions—you're not likely to settle these issues in a single discussion. But do your best to weigh your heart and to set a course for your life and your approach to parenting.

6. *Evaluate your communication with your kids about the things that matter. What would you say you're doing well? How can you improve? If you don't have children, write down and discuss some thoughts on what this might look like.*

7. *What do you think your children are learning about God through your life and your interactions with your spouse? (If you don't have kids, imagine having kids and them watching your daily routine. What would they be learning?)*

8. *How can you teach your kids to see and value the glory of God? Think creatively here. This is a huge and vital aspect of parenting.*

9. *How can you teach your kids about the gospel, not just by what you say, but also in how you live and relate to your kids? This is a huge question, one that you won't resolve in a single conversation. Take it seriously, think imaginatively, and devote as much time to considering it as you can.*

10. *Is there anything about the way you're living in front of your children or teaching them that is actually contrary to the gospel? Ways in which you may be inadvertently teaching your kids the opposite of the gospel? Explain.*

I'm guessing that this last section might have been fairly intense for you. It's not easy to evaluate yourself with that kind of depth. This is one of the truly beautiful aspects of parenting. Not only do we get to care for God's precious children, but it also helps us see more clearly the areas of our lives that still need to be brought into submission to Christ. You will continue to discuss parenting in the next session, but for now, take some time to pray. The task that God has given us as parents would be impossible without the empowering of the Holy Spirit.

11. *Spend some time in prayer. Thank God for the privilege of parenting (if you are not a parent, thank God for the parents who are training up the children all around you). Pray that God would strengthen you and give you wisdom as you seek to honor Him in this aspect of your life.*

REFLECTIONS ON...

What's Really Best for the Kids?

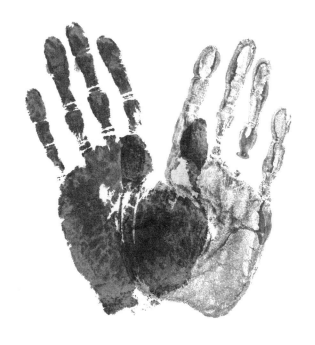

SESSION SEVEN

Raising an Army

For more information on the material in this session,
read Chapter 6 of the book *You & Me Forever*
and take a few minutes to watch the relevant video(s)
at youandmeforever.org. If you read Chapter 6
for the previous session, it might be helpful to at
least glance at the chapter again, perhaps even
rereading it, as a reminder of some of the concepts
you'll discuss in this session.

In this session we are returning again to the topic of parenting. My prayer is that you were challenged in last week's discussion and that God is already working in your heart to better represent Him in your parenting. This session will continue last week's discussion and focus on the mission that God has given us and how that should shape our parenting.

Start by evaluating your overall goal in parenting. What have you been trying to accomplish? What do you hope your children will look like when they are full-grown? What matters most in your parenting? Take some time to consider this and make some notes below.

1. *What would you say has been your highest goal in parenting? Why?*

2. *As you evaluate your actions as a parent, would you say that the goal you iden-tified in the previous question has been reflected in your lifestyle? Or do your choices and actions as a parent reveal a different goal? How so?*

When Jesus rose from the dead and told His followers to make disciples (Matt. 28:18–20), He was setting the agenda for the church. He was establishing the course of history. He was giving orders that govern your personal life, your marriage, and your parenting.

Family is sacred in the church. We place a high value on the family and devote much time and energy to strengthening our families. And we should. But we also need to be careful that our families don't replace God or the mission He has given us. Jesus said some startling words that should make us rethink our interactions with our families:

> "I have come to set a man against his father, and a daughter against her mother, and a daughter-in-law against her mother-in-law. And a person's enemies will be those of his own household.

Whoever loves father or mother more than me is not worthy of me, and whoever loves son or daughter more than me is not worthy of me. And whoever does not take his cross and follow me is not worthy of me. Whoever finds his life will lose it, and whoever loses his life for my sake will find it." (Matthew 10:35–39, emphasis added)

How highly do you value your family? Jesus' words here are strong. This isn't the kind of statement we can take casually. Jesus is saying that if you reach a certain level in loving your family, you can't follow Him! That's terrifying, because I love my family deeply. I can't simply brush this statement aside, saying, "Well, Jesus can't mean…"

At the heart of it, Jesus is saying that our love for Him must eclipse all else. It doesn't matter how amazing your marriage is, how cute your kids are, or how much you enjoy being with them. The point is, if your love for them can be compared to your love for Jesus (see Luke 14:26), then you are not worthy to follow Him. Jesus Himself is the priority in parenting, along with the mission He left for us. We will all need to sacrifice elements of our family life for the sake of the mission. We will have to demonstrate to our children that we love them deeply, but that we love God far more. We will need to teach them to do the same.

3.   *Think deeply about Jesus' words: "Whoever loves son or daughter more than me is not worthy of me." How should this affect your parenting?*

4. *What would it look like to model for your children that God is the most important thing in life? That you love Jesus more than them, and that they should as well?*

The mission that Jesus gave us of making disciples includes our children. We are to make them into disciples. And loving Jesus includes loving our children because He calls us to love and care for them. But it's the mission that takes priority. This is the one thing Jesus called us to do before He returned to the Father. And while we need to make our children into disciples, we also need to train them for the mission of making disciples. Another way to say this is that in making our children into disciples, we will be making them into disciple makers.

It's one thing to tell our children that God's mission is important. It's another thing to demonstrate that the mission is important. To ingrain the mission in them. To shape your life in light of the mission and allow your children to see firsthand that nothing is more important, challenging, or rewarding than the mission that God has left for us. This will mean modeling service and discipleship for your children. They should be able to look at your life and know experientially what it looks like to die to self and serve others. It should also mean finding ways for your children to serve. It's often quicker and easier to do things yourself; you may even feel good about serving your children by doing everything for them. But if they are going to learn to be servants, you need to be finding ways for them to actively serve others.

You have already considered what it would look like to shape your marriage with God's mission in view. Now take some time to think about how your children can be incorporated into this as well.

5. *How can you raise your children to understand and live for the mission? Be creative with your response.*

6. *What would it look like to raise kids who know how to serve as Christ served? What are some opportunities to serve that you can give your kids?*

7. *In what ways are you modeling service for your children, not only in your home, but in your church and community as well? If you're not doing this, how do you think this is affecting your children?*

One major obstacle to God-honoring parenting is fear. Actually, fear undermines much of what God calls us to do in every area of life. Perhaps you're afraid that your children won't love you in return. Maybe you're afraid that your children will be hurt if you involve them in reaching out and serving. You may be afraid of your children growing up to be rebellious or godless. But as terrifying as parenting can be, we can't parent out of fear.

When Paul wrote to instruct Timothy regarding his ministry, he called him to "fan into flame the gift of God." Timothy seems to have been afraid of pursuing God's calling to the fullest extent, because Paul reminded him, "God gave us a spirit not of fear but of power and love and self-control" (2 Tim. 1:6–7). It can be terrifying to serve God in the face of difficulty, so Paul reminded Timothy that although he was afraid, God gave us a spirit of power, not fear. And if we are truly motivated by love for God and love for our children, we need to remember that "there is no fear in love, but perfect love casts out fear" (1 John 4:18).

As a parent, it's difficult to see our children struggle. We'd prefer to shield them from the trials of life. So intentionally placing our children in the path of mockery, persecution, and self-denial does not come naturally. But we need to be reminded of James' words that trials should be a cause for rejoicing because they produce character and make us into mature people who lack nothing (James 1:2–4). We need to believe this for ourselves, and we need to believe it for our children as well. If we want them to become mature adults, shielding our children from God's mission and keeping them from all potential trials is the worst possible approach.

8. *How have you seen fear affect parenting (your own or someone else's)? In these situations, what would the biblical alternative look like?*

9. *How should James 1:2–4 affect our parenting? What does it really mean to raise strong kids?*

By this point, you're probably recognizing how difficult parenting is. If you're a parent, you knew that before you picked up this book. The reality is, parenting is impossible. We're called to lead kids into loving and imitating Jesus—that's not something we can do. And this is why prayer is so important. Ultimately, they are not *our* kids. They belong to God. He loves them more than we ever could. He knows what they are capable of and what plans He has for their lives. If God has entrusted children to your care, then you need to take that responsibility seriously. But you cannot forget that you are raising those children for God's kingdom, not your own.

The most powerful thing we can do for our kids is pray for them. If we are going to raise up an army of children who will go into the world and transform it for the glory of God, we will need to be on our knees. Take some time to evaluate your prayer for your children. Once you've discussed this, close out this session by praying together—for yourselves as parents, for the parents in your group, and for your children.

10. Discuss your prayers for your children. How often do you pray for them? What kinds of things do you pray for? Why do you think this matters?

11. How can you improve in praying for your kids? If you don't have kids, discuss how you would like to pray for your kids and why.

12. *Spend some time in prayer. Ask God to continue to form your mind and shape your life with His truth and for His mission. Pray for your kids and for the parents in your group. Ask God to raise up the next generation to be an army for His kingdom, and pray that God would empower your generation of parents to be used by God in training these kids for His mission.*

REFLECTIONS ON...

Raising an Army

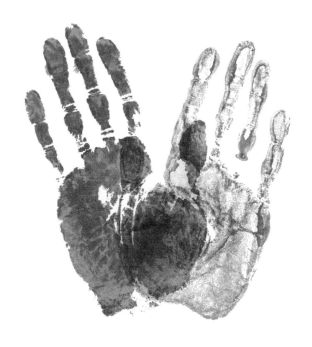

SESSION EIGHT

The Amazing Race

For more information on the material in this session,
read Chapter 7 of the book *You & Me Forever*
and take a few minutes to watch the relevant
video(s) at youandmeforever.org.

As you come now to the final session of this study, it's time to reflect on the ground you've covered and think about what will happen next. We have all experienced Bible studies that feel so profound and challenging, yet a month or two down the road we find that we haven't changed at all.

This has always been a danger for anyone who reads the Bible. James had to warn his readers that learning is not enough: "But be doers of the word, and not hearers only, deceiving yourselves" (James 1:22). Paul warned that knowledge without love merely puffs us up (1 Cor. 8:1). John urged his readers to do more than talk about love:

> If anyone has the world's goods and sees his brother in need, yet closes his heart against him, how does God's love abide in him? Little children, let us not love in word or talk but in deed and in truth. (1 John 3:17–18)

Anytime we contemplate a concept as rich as marriage, we're bound to gain new insights. But if all you do is gain a better understanding of marriage, or develop a longer wish list of what you'd like your marriage to look like, or accumulate more ammunition for looking down on all of the people around you with bad marriages, then you've missed the point. If you're not changing, you've wasted your time.

Actually, if you are not changing in response to what you've learned, putting these truths into practical action, then this study has actually been harmful to your soul. Accumulating knowledge without putting it into practice is a form of pride, and it can devour your soul. The test for whether this study has had a positive or harmful effect on you is where you go from here. If you grow in humility, service, love for God and His mission, etc., then this has been a good study. If you grow more intelligent and your life and marriage remain the same, this has been a step backward in your Christian life.

Paul compares the Christian life to a race and his pursuit of Christ to training:

> Do you not know that in a race all the runners run, but only one receives the prize? So run that you may obtain it. Every athlete exercises self-control in all things. They do it to receive a perishable wreath, but we an imperishable. So I do not run aimlessly; I do not box as one beating the air. But I discipline my body and keep it under control, lest after preaching to others I myself should be disqualified. (1 Corinthians 9:24–27)

You looked at this passage in an earlier session, but I want you to think about it again. Knowing the rules of the race is different than actually running it. Running the race requires training, discipline, and perseverance. I see too many Christians wasting their lives on everything but the mission that God gave them. We need to see this life as a race, and devote our energy toward that end.

1. *In 1 Corinthians 9:24–27, Paul compares the Christian life to a race. Describe some of the ways in which this analogy is fitting—profound, even.*

2. *Continuing with Paul's race analogy, how should your marriage be seen as a race? How might this affect the way you view your marriage?*

Many Christians treat the Christian life as a sprint, and all of the emphasis is placed on how one begins the race. But the race is more of a marathon, though we are never sure how long the race will last. When you run a marathon, you want to run the second half of the race even faster than the first, and sprint as you near the finish line. You may be reading this as you prepare for marriage, in the midst of your marriage, or toward the end of the your life. Regardless of your stage of life, you need to be picking up the pace. It doesn't matter how well you started the race; it matters how you finish.

In Joshua 14:6–15, we find Caleb in his later years. He was 40 when he spied out the Promised Land and, along with Joshua, boldly told the people of Israel that God could easily give the land to them. Now Caleb is 85, and he's begging Joshua to give him the hill country so he can drive out the wicked inhabitants and claim more of the Promised Land. I encourage your to read this story in your Bible right now. It will take you less than five minutes, and it's well worth it.

I love that we have this picture of Caleb finishing strong. He wasn't satisfied with what he had done in the past, nor did he let his age change his pursuits. If we find ourselves "settling in" with life or marriage, or if there are certain comforts or routines we aren't willing to let go of for the sake of the mission, it means that we have turned around and are running in the opposite direction. Take some time to consider how your race is going and how your marriage ties into this.

3. *The goal is to finish the race strong, running even faster than we did at the beginning. As you look back at your life and marriage to this point, what mistakes would you say you've made that have "slowed you down"? These may be bad things, or they could be good things that distracted you from better things. (If you are not married, discuss mistakes you have seen others make that you'd like to avoid.)*

4. *As you look forward to what remains of the race, how do you plan to change or further develop your marriage to make the end of your race even stronger than the beginning?*

It breaks my heart to see Christian marriages derailed. Here are couples who began pursuing God's mission, but ended up distracted and sidelined. What was an opportunity to serve God more effectively turned into a pursuit of personal happiness. What should have been an environment of mutual support for reaching out to a hurting world degenerated into bitter fights and mutual attacks.

The destruction of Christian marriages is sad, not because it signals the end of a person's dreams of happiness, but because it dismantles a potentially fruitful means of building God's kingdom. It turns a beautiful picture of God's grace in this world into yet another excuse to slander God's people as weak and worldly.

Take some time to consider the pursuits, mindsets, and practices that tend to derail marriages and discuss why this matters so much.

5. *How have you seen marriages derailed? This could be personal examples from your own marriage, or it could be observations of other people's marriages. Avoid gossiping or insulting others. Instead, focus on the pitfalls and discuss how these can be avoided in your own marriage.*

As we discussed in a previous session, the rewards that God offers us are beyond compare. We actually get to spend eternity with God, in His presence, with all of the blessings and rewards He can bestow on us! Yet we are so quick to trade in those promises for self-made substitutes. Rather than hoping in God's promises for eternity, we try to build our version of heaven on earth. We try to make our spouses into saviors and our marriages into mini-heavens that will make us happy.

Until we see something greater at stake in our marriages than our own happiness, our marriages will look nothing like God's intention. What God offers us is infinitely better, but we don't believe, we don't wait patiently, we don't obey. Evaluate your marriage once again in light of God's promises about the future. Honestly assess where you are hoping to find your happiness. Try to make your marriage into everything it should be without trying to make it be what it shouldn't be.

6. *In what sense can marriage and family become a substitute for God's promises of heaven? How do we try to make marriage into a little "heaven on earth"? Have you seen or experienced any examples of this?*

7. *How can you enjoy marriage while avoiding the idolatrous and heaven-replacing nature it often takes on?*

Finish off this session by taking stock of what you've learned and where you're going. This will in some ways be a review of your previous discussions, but take this opportunity to put the pieces together. As you look back over everything you've covered, how would you summarize where you've come and where you want to be headed?

8. *What would you say has been the most helpful and/or challenging insight you've picked up during the course of this study? Why do you say that?*

9. *How are you going to respond to this study? Spend time talking with your spouse about how all of this should affect your marriage from here on out. This could be a simple review of the many things you've discussed and resolved to do throughout the study. Or perhaps some new thoughts are developing. Pray and discuss this with your spouse, and if you are working through this material with a group, share your thoughts and plans with your group to spur more ideas.*

10. *Spend an extended time in prayer. Don't let this be just another Bible study. Beg God to change your heart, life, and marriage in light of His truth. Pray that He would take your marriage and use it in powerful and unexpected ways for the sake of His mission and His glory.*

NOTES FOR DISCUSSION LEADERS

A small group working through this material will benefit from having a discussion leader. If that's you, don't worry: you don't need to have all the answers. This workbook is discussion-driven, not teacher-driven. All you need is the willingness to prepare each week, guide the discussion, and rely on the Holy Spirit to work in your heart and the hearts of group members. This study can give you hands-on experience in depending not on your natural leadership abilities but on the Spirit. If you pray for His help, He will give it.

Discussion Leader's Job Description

The discussion leader's job isn't to have all the answers. He or she simply needs to:

+ *Keep the group on track when it's tempted to go off on a tangent.*

+ *Keep the discussion moving so that it doesn't get stuck on one question.*

+ *Make sure that everyone gets a chance to talk and that no one dominates. (It is not necessary that every person respond aloud to every question, but every person should have the chance to do so.)*

+ *Make sure that the discussion remains respectful.*

Preparing for the Discussion

As the discussion leader, you'll want to read the appropriate chapter from *You & Me Forever* before each session. I would also recommend watching the corresponding video ahead of time. Try to work through your own responses to the discussion questions ahead of time as well. Just before the meeting, be sure the chairs are arranged so that everyone can see each other's faces.

Guiding the Discussion

A few ground rules can make the discussion deeper:

+ *Confidentiality: Whatever is said in the group stays in the group. Nothing is to be repeated to those who weren't there.*

+ *Honesty: We're not here to impress each other. We're here to grow and to get to know each other better.*

+ *Respect: Disagreement is welcome. Disrespect is not.*

The discussion should be a conversation among the group members, not a one-on-one with the leader. You can encourage this with statements like, "Thanks, Allison. What do others of you think?" or "Does anyone have a similar experience, or a different one?"

Don't be afraid of silence—it means group members are thinking about how to answer a question. Trust that the Spirit is working in the members of your group, and wait. Sometimes it's helpful to rephrase the question in your own words. Then wait for others' responses, and avoid jumping in with your own.

We recommend discussing the numbered questions in order. Read each question aloud and ask the group to respond. Even if an answer seems obvious, have a few people share their thoughts—you never know what will spark a challenging conversation. As you work through the questions, feel free to read a section out loud if the group is unclear on what a question is getting at.

You can choose to have the group members watch the videos for each session (available at youandmeforever.org) on their own before the group meeting, or you can choose to watch them during your group time. If you choose to watch them together, we recommend watching the videos at the beginning of your group time to prompt more discussion.

We decided not to include a "leader's guide" that gives answers to each of the questions mainly because the most profitable aspect of studying this material in a group is the discussion itself. The destination is important, but you can't get there without the journey. Where specific answers are required, we have tried to point you toward the Scriptures. The answer may not always jump out at you, but at the very least your discussion will be headed in the right direction.

The answers are important, but we are most concerned that people may study God and never *know* Him, never be *changed* by Him. And when it comes to marriage, we are concerned that people will gain lofty ideals for their marriage, but never put them into practice. With every session, keep asking yourself and your group: "How should this change us? If we really submitted our lives to Jesus and opened ourselves up to the power of the Holy Spirit, what would He have us do, where would He have us go?" At the end of the day, it's about laying hold of the power of the Spirit in order to accomplish what God has placed us on this earth to do. It's about advancing the kingdom of God. It's about His will being done on earth as in heaven.

Most of all, spend time praying for your group. You can't talk anyone into a wholehearted devotion to God. You can't *convince* couples to have healthy marriages. Pray that the Spirit of God would fill your lives and do the impossible in and through you. In the book of Acts, the human actors were just ordinary, weak people, but the Holy Spirit accomplished unbelievable things through these ordinary people as they prayed and submitted themselves to following His leading. May God accomplish the extraordinary in your lives and through your marriages as you seek to follow Jesus with everything you've got.